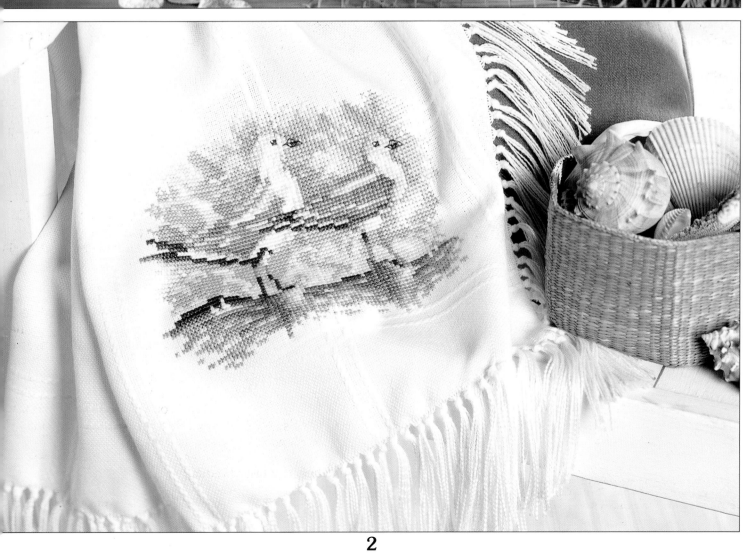

3

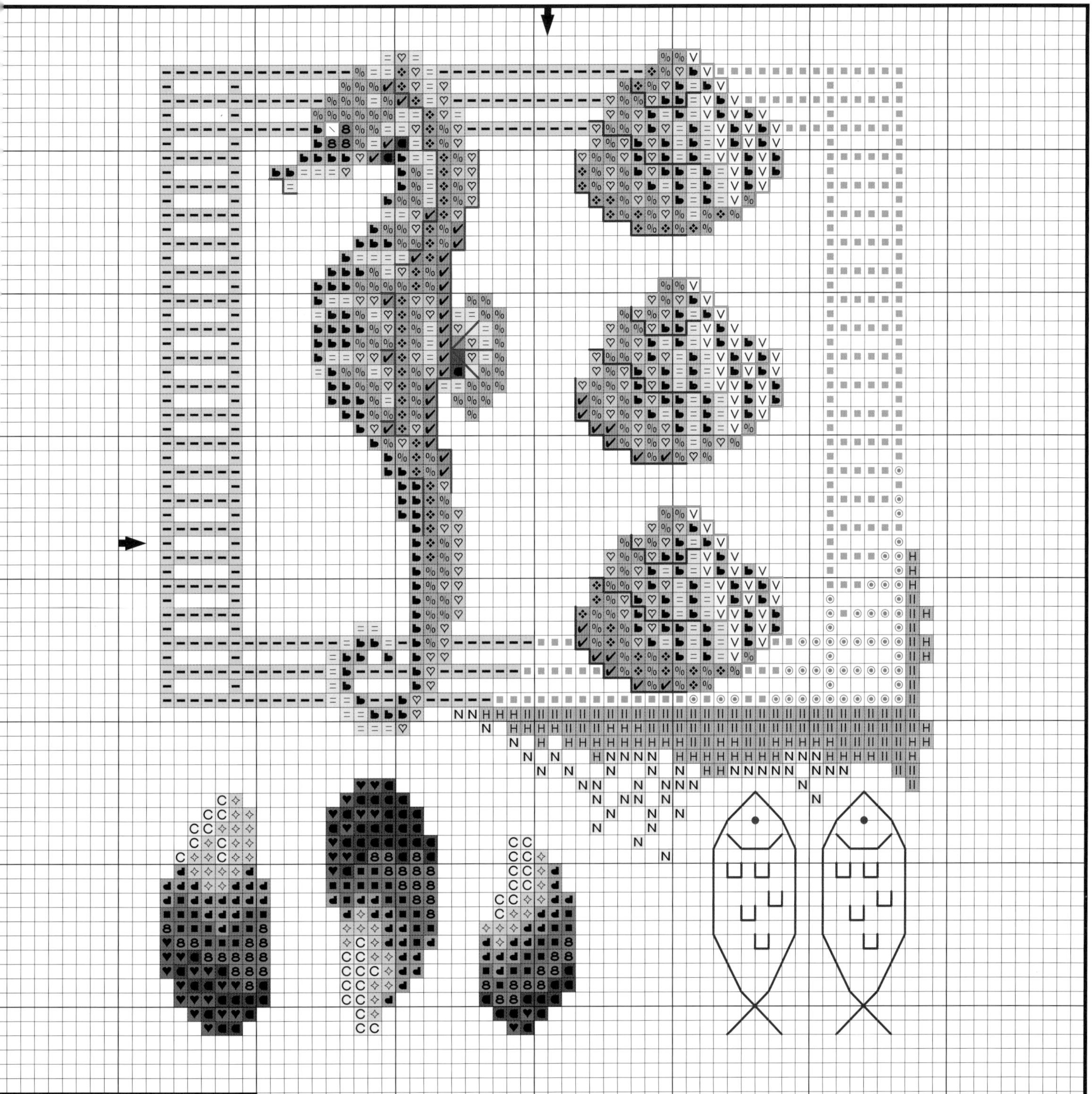

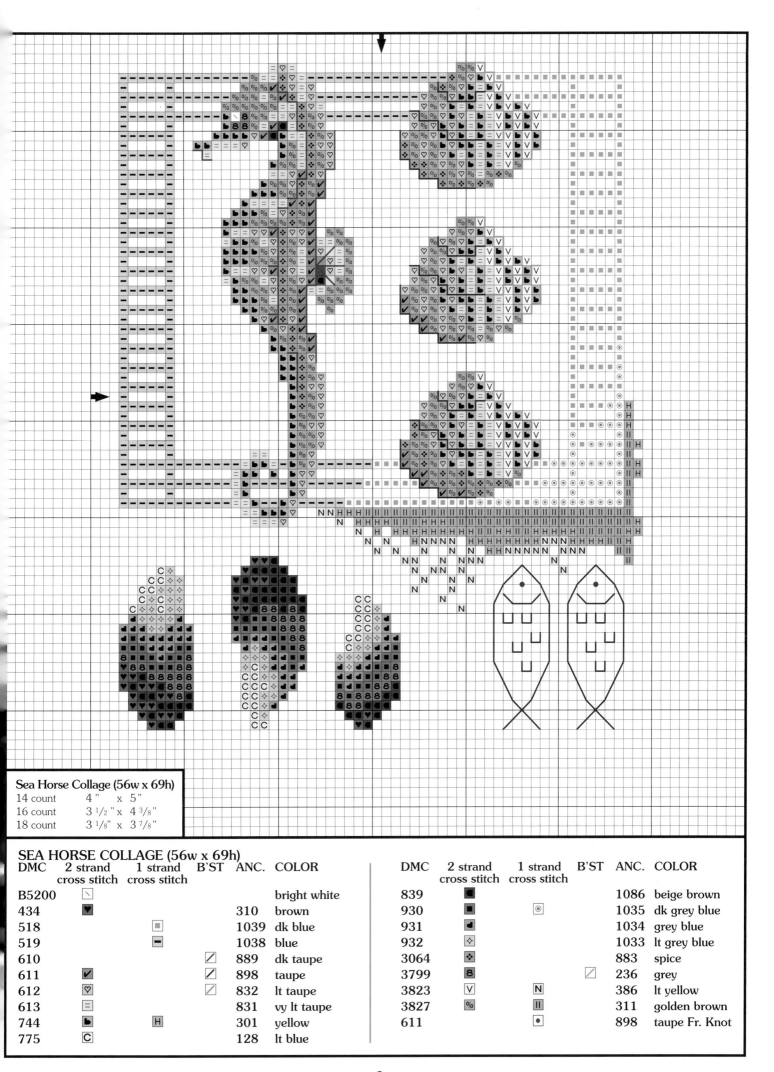

Sea Horse Collage (56w x 69h)

14 count	4 "	x	5 "
16 count	3 1/2 "	x	4 3/8 "
18 count	3 1/8 "	x	3 7/8 "

SEA HORSE COLLAGE (56w x 69h)

DMC	2 strand cross stitch	1 strand cross stitch	B'ST	ANC.	COLOR
B5200	⟍				bright white
434	♥			310	brown
518		▫		1039	dk blue
519		▬		1038	blue
610			/	889	dk taupe
611	✔		/	898	taupe
612	♡		/	832	lt taupe
613	=			831	vy lt taupe
744	◣	H		301	yellow
775	C			128	lt blue
839	◖			1086	beige brown
930	■	◉		1035	dk grey blue
931	◗			1034	grey blue
932	✧			1033	lt grey blue
3064	✣			883	spice
3799	8		/	236	grey
3823	V	N		386	lt yellow
3827	%	II		311	golden brown
611		•		898	taupe Fr. Knot

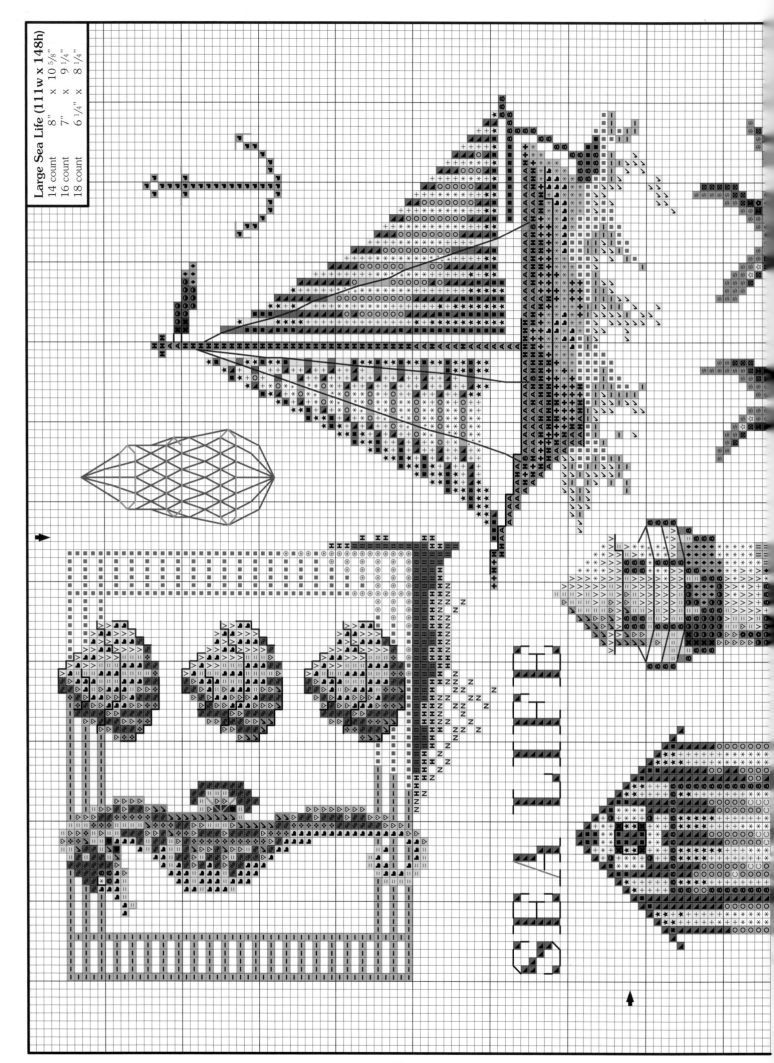

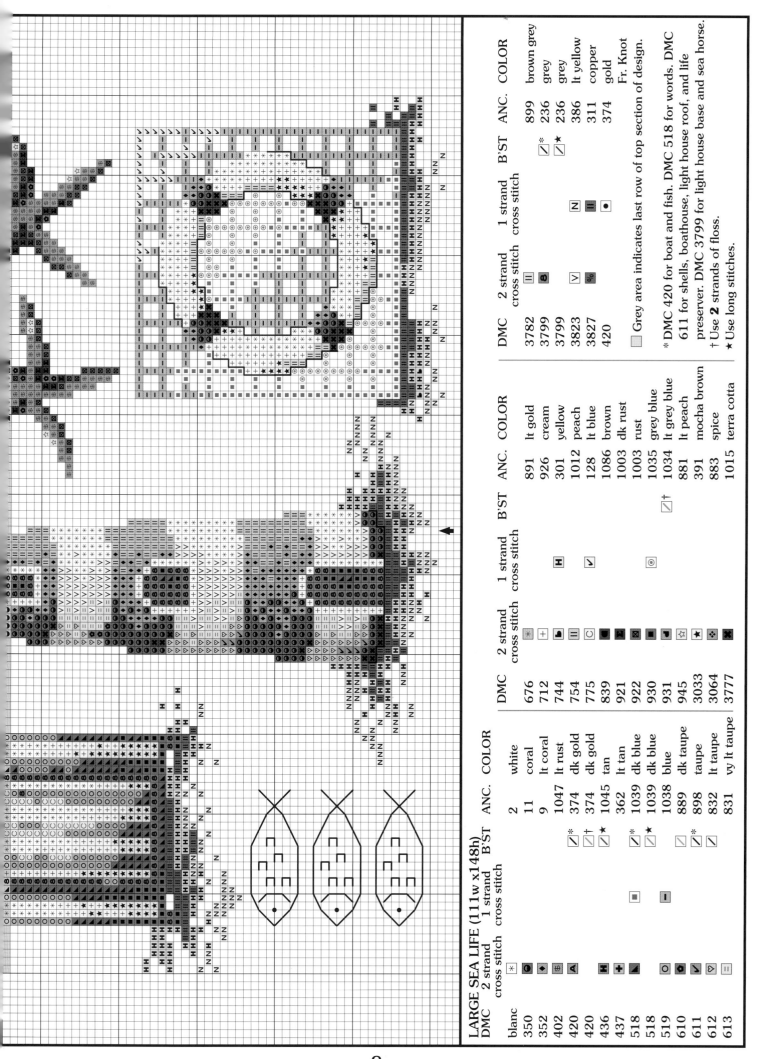

LARGE SEA LIFE (111w x148h)

DMC	2 strand cross stitch	1 strand cross stitch	B'ST	ANC.	COLOR
blanc	✱			2	white
350	◐			11	coral
352	◆			9	lt coral
402	#			1047	lt rust
420	▲		◢*	374	dk gold
420			◢†	374	dk gold
436	⊞		◢★	1045	tan
437	✚			362	lt tan
518	◣		◢*	1039	dk blue
518			★	1039	dk blue
519	◙		◢	1038	blue
610	◉		◢*	889	dk taupe
611	◩		◢	898	taupe
612	▷			832	lt taupe
613	⹀			831	vy lt taupe

DMC	2 strand cross stitch	1 strand cross stitch	B'ST	ANC.	COLOR
676	✳			891	lt gold
712	+			926	cream
744	◣			301	yellow
754	▦			1012	peach
775	○			128	lt blue
839	◪			1086	brown
921	⬕	H		1003	dk rust
922	⊠			1003	rust
930	■	↴		1035	grey blue
931	◩		◢†	1034	lt grey blue
945	☆			881	lt peach
3033	★	⊙		391	mocha brown
3064	✦			883	spice
3777	✕			1015	terra cotta

DMC	2 strand cross stitch	1 strand cross stitch	B'ST	ANC.	COLOR
3782	=			899	brown grey
3799	▧		◢*	236	grey
3799		N	◢★	236	grey
3823	▽			386	lt yellow
3827	⁒	⊞		311	copper
420		●		374	gold
					Fr. Knot

▨ Grey area indicates last row of top section of design.

* DMC 420 for boat and fish. DMC 518 for words. DMC 611 for shells, boathouse, light house roof, and life preserver. DMC 3799 for light house base and sea horse.
† Use **2** strands of floss.
★ Use long stitches.

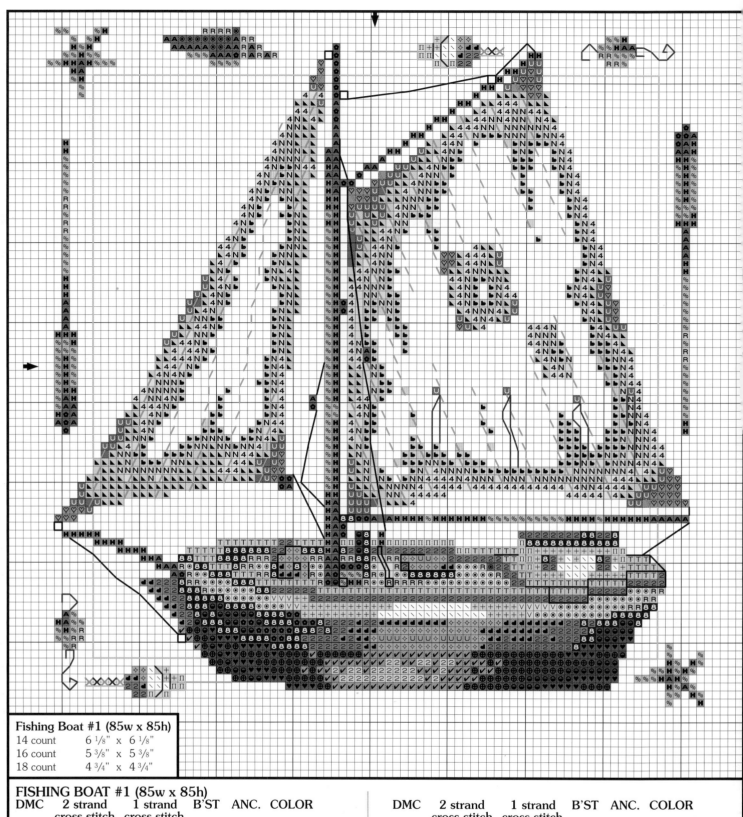

Fishing Boat #1 (85w x 85h)

14 count	6 1/8"	x 6 1/8"
16 count	5 3/8"	x 5 3/8"
18 count	4 3/4"	x 4 3/4"

FISHING BOAT #1 (85w x 85h)

DMC	2 strand cross stitch	1 strand cross stitch	B'ST	ANC.	COLOR
B5200	◻				bright white
317	2		╱*	400	lt grey
420	A		╱†	374	hazel brown
436	H	♥		1045	tan
610	⬟		╱	889	taupe
632	♥			936	spice
676	R	◣	╱*	891	gold
677	◉	4		886	lt gold
712	+	◩	╱	926	cream
927	T		╱	848	blue grey
931	◧			1034	grey blue
932	◇			1033	lt grey blue
3045	◉	U	╱†	888	lt hazel brown

DMC	2 strand cross stitch	1 strand cross stitch	B'ST	ANC.	COLOR
3072	Π			847	beaver grey
3753	U			1031	blue
3778	✔			1013	terra cotta
3779	2			1012	lt terra cotta
3781	◉			904	mocha brown
3799	8		╱★	236	pewter grey
3823	V	N		386	yellow
3827	%			311	golden brown
3830	⊕		╱	5975	dk terra cotta

*DMC 317 for fishing tackle (**2** strands). DMC 676 for sails.
†DMC 420 for fishing tackle (**2** strands). DMC 3045 for sail.
★Use long stitches for rigging.

9

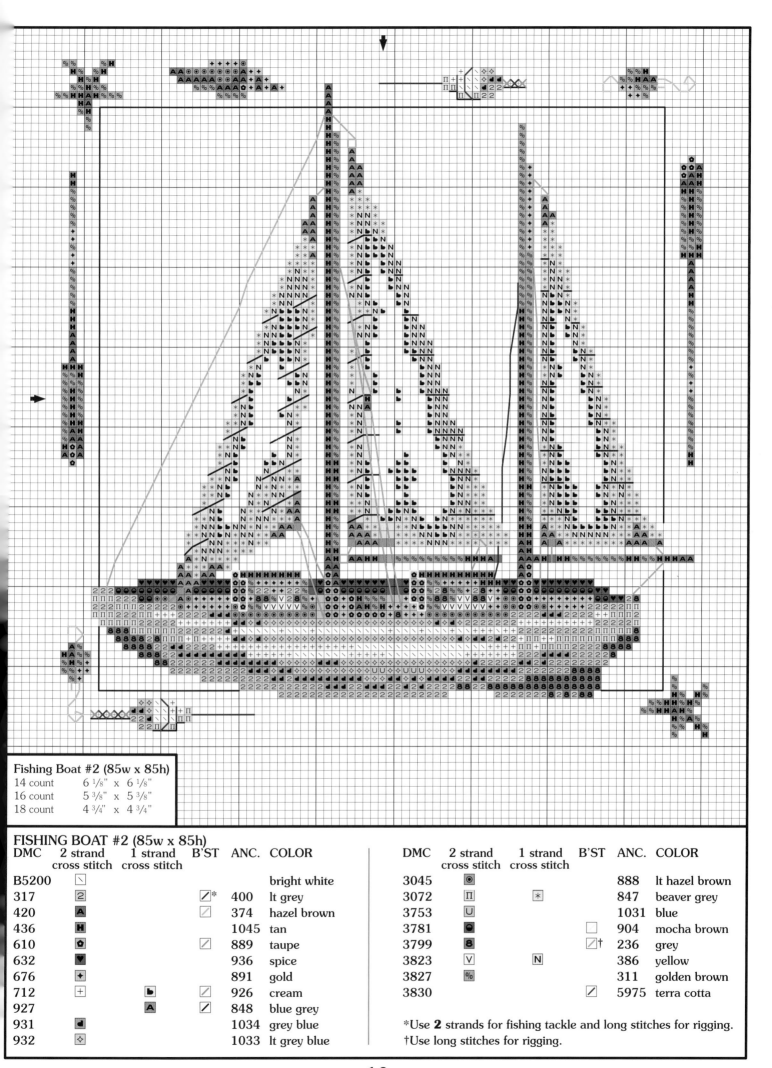

Fishing Boat #2 (85w x 85h)

14 count	6 1/8" x 6 1/8"	
16 count	5 3/8" x 5 3/8"	
18 count	4 3/4" x 4 3/4"	

FISHING BOAT #2 (85w x 85h)

DMC	2 strand cross stitch	1 strand cross stitch	B'ST	ANC.	COLOR
B5200	◣				bright white
317	2		◸*	400	lt grey
420	A		◸	374	hazel brown
436	H			1045	tan
610	✿		◸	889	taupe
632	♥			936	spice
676	✦			891	gold
712	+	◗	◸	926	cream
927		A	◸	848	blue grey
931	◣			1034	grey blue
932	◇			1033	lt grey blue

DMC	2 strand cross stitch	1 strand cross stitch	B'ST	ANC.	COLOR
3045	◉			888	lt hazel brown
3072	∏	*		847	beaver grey
3753	U			1031	blue
3781	◕		□	904	mocha brown
3799	8		◸†	236	grey
3823	V	N		386	yellow
3827	%			311	golden brown
3830			◸	5975	terra cotta

*Use **2** strands for fishing tackle and long stitches for rigging.
†Use long stitches for rigging.

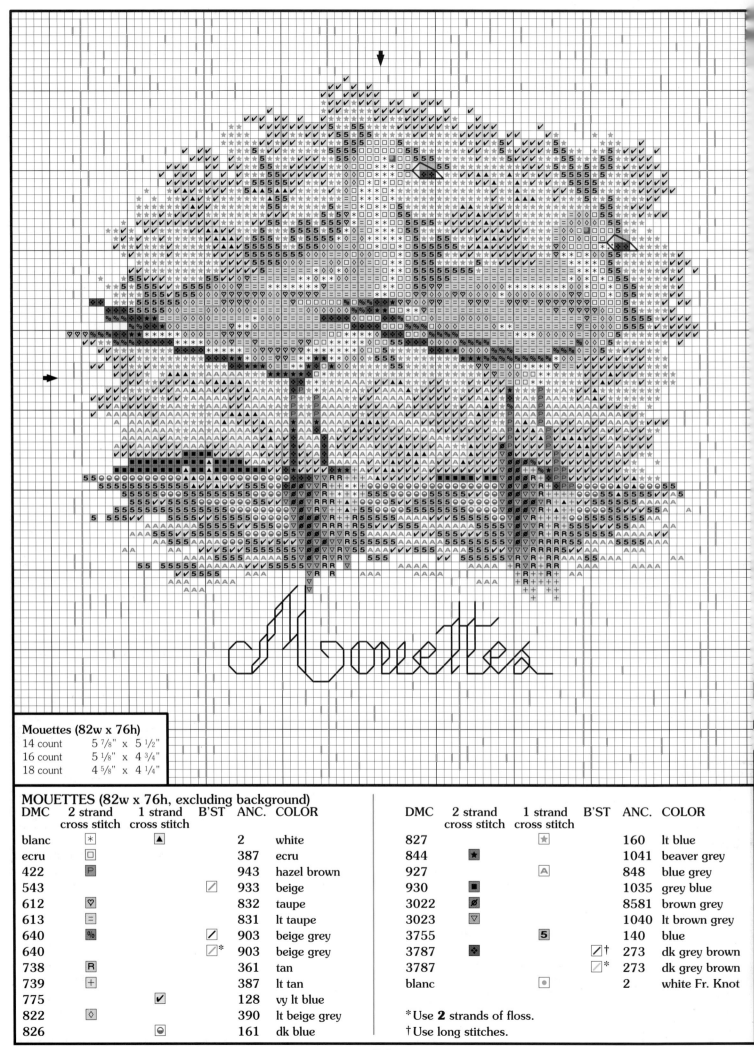

Mouettes (82w x 76h)

14 count	5 7/8"	x 5 1/2"
16 count	5 1/8"	x 4 3/4"
18 count	4 5/8"	x 4 1/4"

MOUETTES (82w x 76h, excluding background)

DMC	2 strand cross stitch	1 strand cross stitch	B'ST	ANC.	COLOR
blanc	✻	▲		2	white
ecru	▢			387	ecru
422	P			943	hazel brown
543		╱		933	beige
612	▽			832	taupe
613	═			831	lt taupe
640	%	╱		903	beige grey
640		╱*		903	beige grey
738	R			361	tan
739	+			387	lt tan
775		✔		128	vy lt blue
822	◇			390	lt beige grey
826		◉		161	dk blue

DMC	2 strand cross stitch	1 strand cross stitch	B'ST	ANC.	COLOR
827		★		160	lt blue
844	★			1041	beaver grey
927		A		848	blue grey
930	■			1035	grey blue
3022	∅			8581	brown grey
3023	▽			1040	lt brown grey
3755			5	140	blue
3787	✷		╱†	273	dk grey brown
3787			╱*	273	dk grey brown
blanc		⦿		2	white Fr. Knot

*Use **2** strands of floss.
†Use long stitches.

11

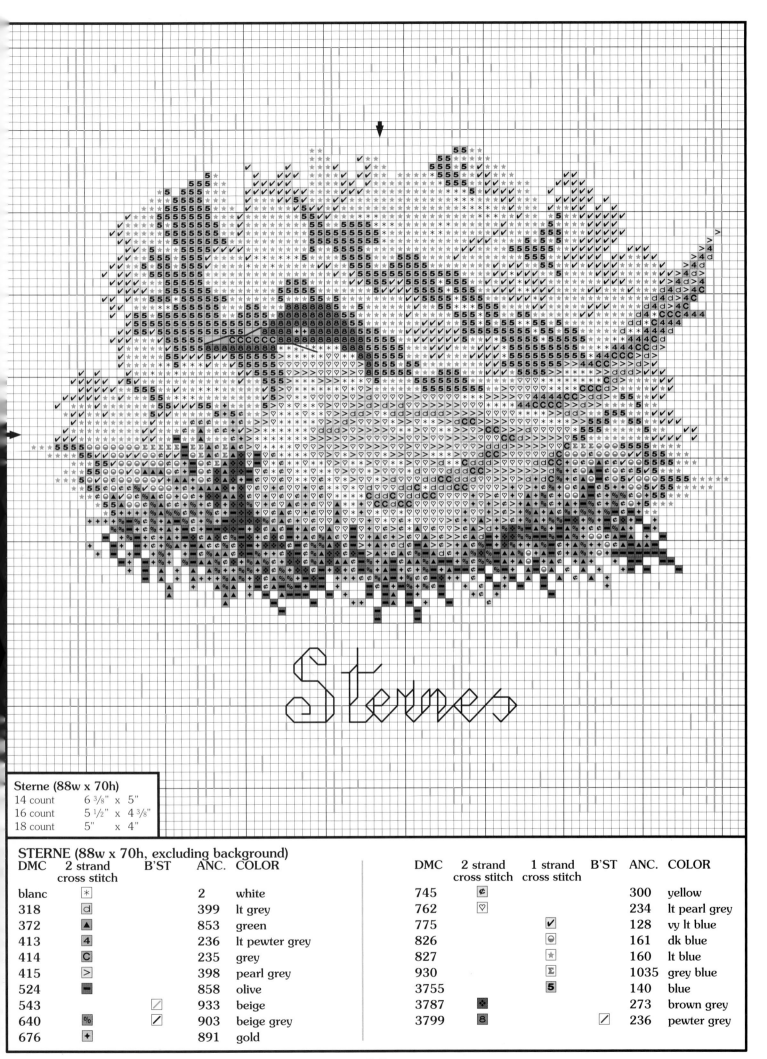

Sterne (88w x 70h)

14 count	6 3/8"	x	5"
16 count	5 1/2"	x	4 3/8"
18 count	5"	x	4"

STERNE (88w x 70h, excluding background)

DMC	2 strand cross stitch	B'ST	ANC.	COLOR
blanc	✳		2	white
318	d		399	lt grey
372	▲		853	green
413	4		236	lt pewter grey
414	C		235	grey
415	>		398	pearl grey
524	▬		858	olive
543		╱	933	beige
640	%	╱	903	beige grey
676	✦		891	gold

DMC	2 strand cross stitch	1 strand cross stitch	B'ST	ANC.	COLOR
745	¢			300	yellow
762	♡			234	lt pearl grey
775			✔	128	vy lt blue
826		◉		161	dk blue
827		★		160	lt blue
930		Σ		1035	grey blue
3755		5		140	blue
3787	❖			273	brown grey
3799	8		╱	236	pewter grey

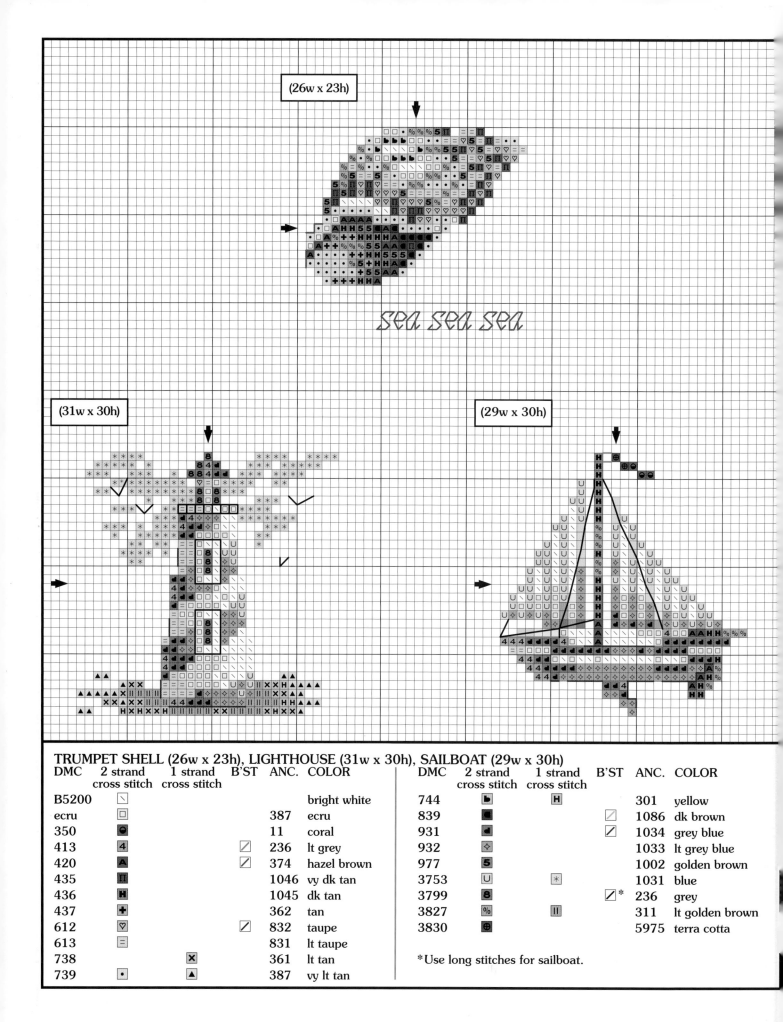

(26w x 23h)

sea sea sea

(31w x 30h)

(29w x 30h)

TRUMPET SHELL (26w x 23h), LIGHTHOUSE (31w x 30h), SAILBOAT (29w x 30h)

DMC	2 strand cross stitch	1 strand cross stitch	B'ST	ANC.	COLOR
B5200	◣				bright white
ecru	◻			387	ecru
350	◕			11	coral
413	4		◪	236	lt grey
420	▲		◪	374	hazel brown
435	Π			1046	vy dk tan
436	H			1045	dk tan
437	✚			362	tan
612	♡		◪	832	taupe
613	=			831	lt taupe
738		✖		361	lt tan
739	•	▲		387	vy lt tan

DMC	2 strand cross stitch	1 strand cross stitch	B'ST	ANC.	COLOR
744	◗	H		301	yellow
839	◼		◪	1086	dk brown
931	◣		◪	1034	grey blue
932	◈			1033	lt grey blue
977	5			1002	golden brown
3753	U	✳		1031	blue
3799	8		◪*	236	grey
3827	%	Ⅱ		311	lt golden brown
3830	⊕			5975	terra cotta

*Use long stitches for sailboat.

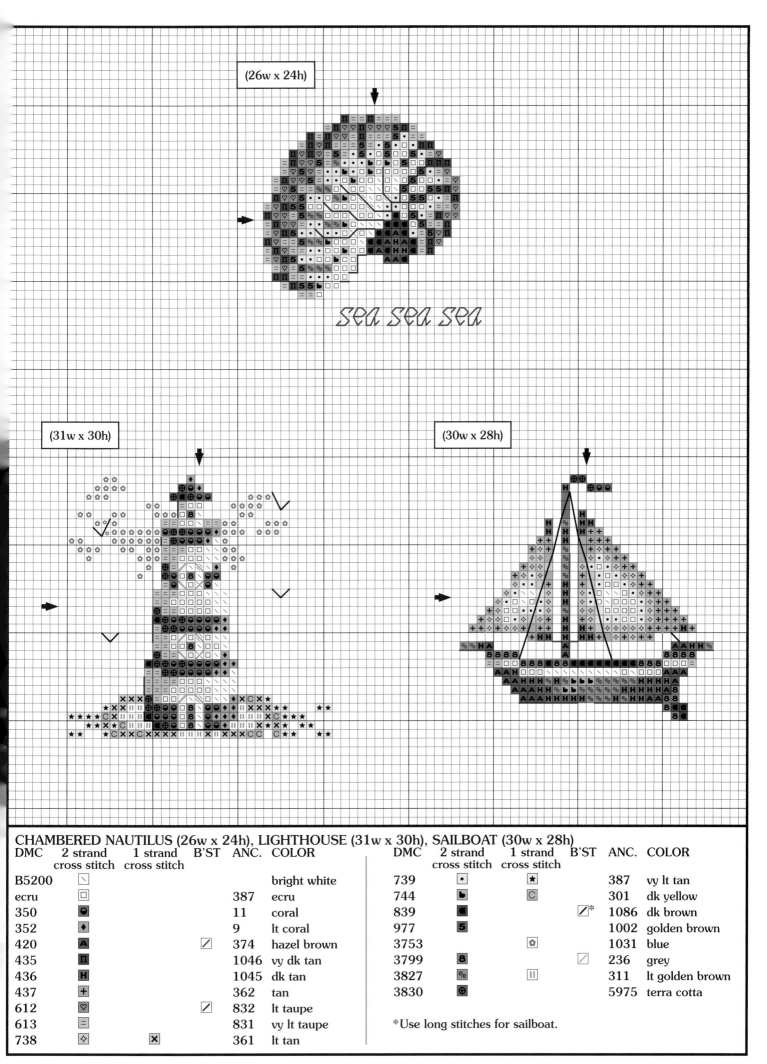

sea sea sea

(26w x 24h)

(31w x 30h)

(30w x 28h)

CHAMBERED NAUTILUS (26w x 24h), LIGHTHOUSE (31w x 30h), SAILBOAT (30w x 28h)

DMC	2 strand cross stitch	1 strand cross stitch	B'ST	ANC.	COLOR	DMC	2 strand cross stitch	1 strand cross stitch	B'ST	ANC.	COLOR
B5200	◹				bright white	739	•	★		387	vy lt tan
ecru	▢			387	ecru	744	◣	C		301	dk yellow
350	◖			11	coral	839	◼		◿*	1086	dk brown
352	◆			9	lt coral	977	5			1002	golden brown
420	A		◿	374	hazel brown	3753		⬠		1031	blue
435	Π			1046	vy dk tan	3799	8		◿	236	grey
436	H			1045	dk tan	3827	%	‖		311	lt golden brown
437	+			362	tan	3830	⊕			5975	terra cotta
612	♡		◿	832	lt taupe						
613	=			831	vy lt taupe	*Use long stitches for sailboat.					
738	◇	X		361	lt tan						

14

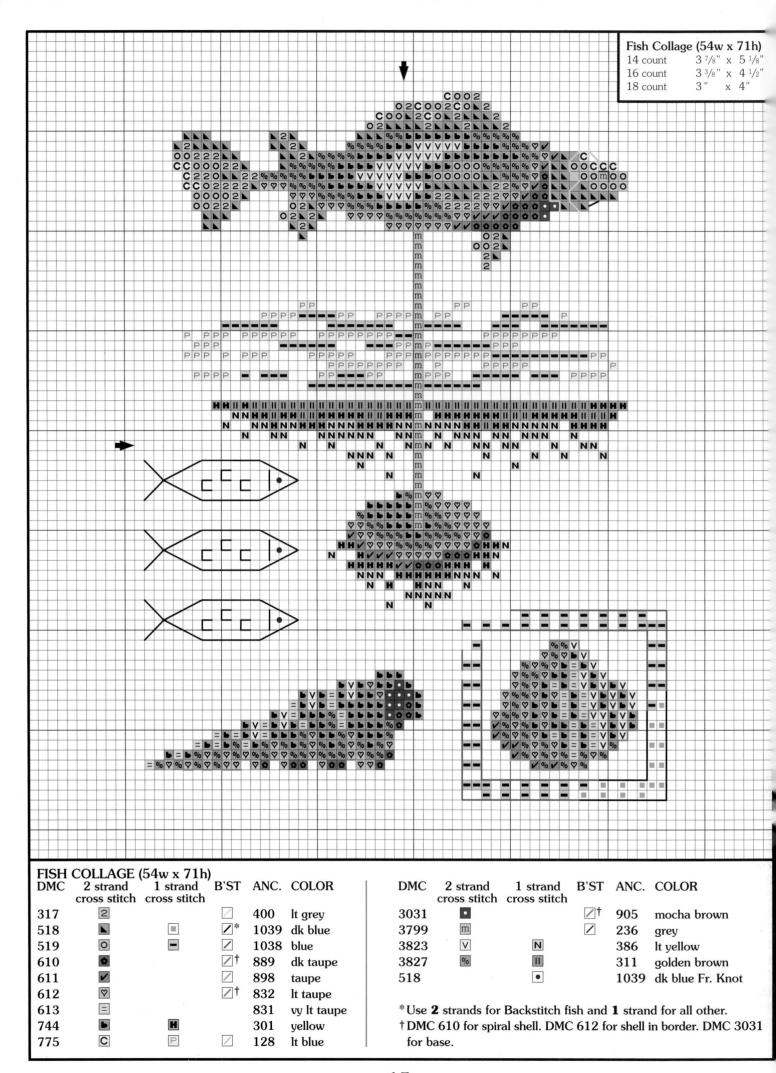

Fish Collage (54w x 71h)

14 count	3 7/8" x 5 1/8"
16 count	3 3/8" x 4 1/2"
18 count	3" x 4"

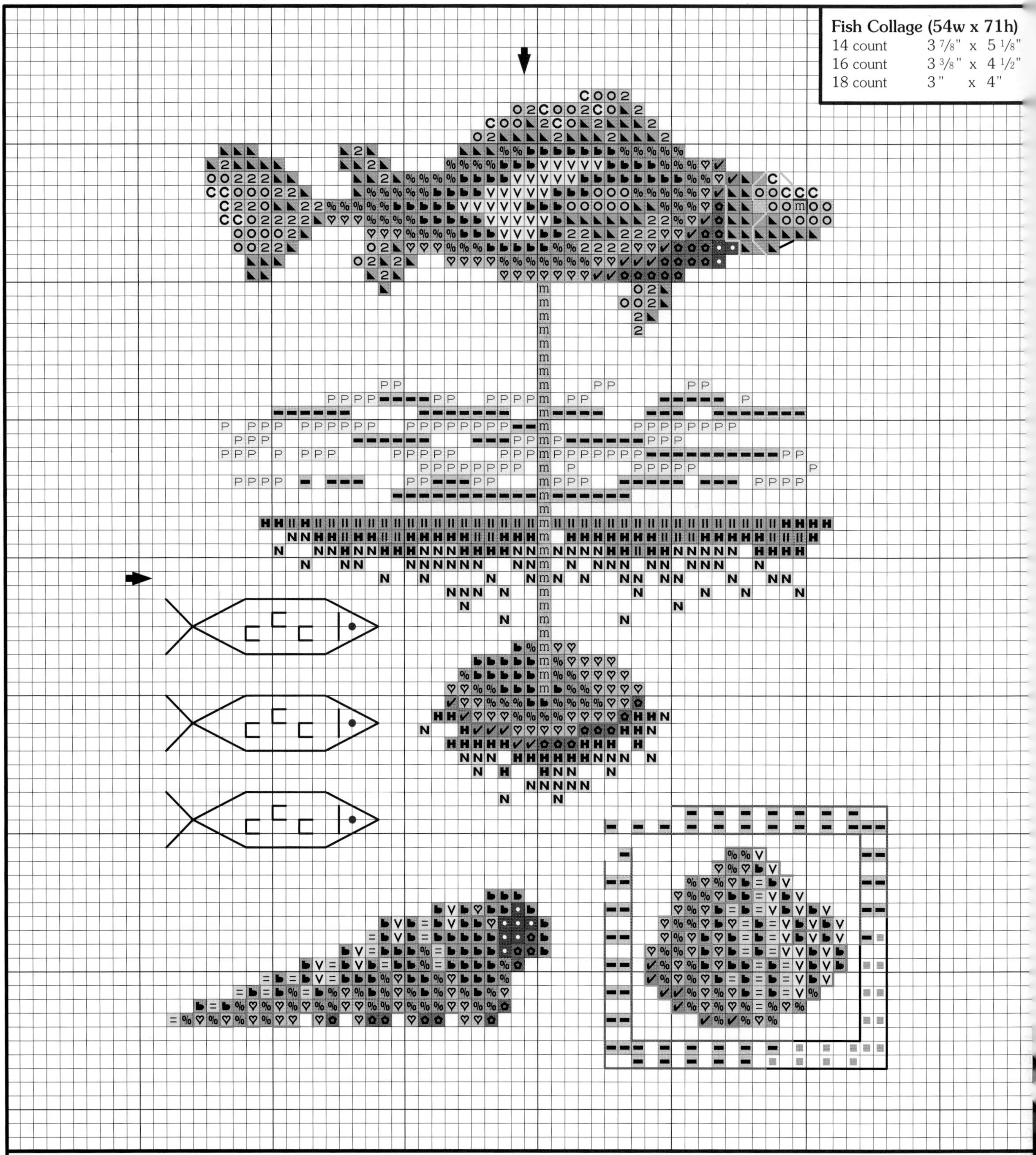

FISH COLLAGE (54w x 71h)

DMC	2 strand cross stitch	1 strand cross stitch	B'ST	ANC.	COLOR
317	2		/	400	lt grey
518	◣	■	/ *	1039	dk blue
519	O	−	/	1038	blue
610	✿		/ †	889	dk taupe
611	✓		/	898	taupe
612	♡		/ †	832	lt taupe
613	=			831	vy lt taupe
744	▶	H		301	yellow
775	C	P	/	128	lt blue
3031	•		/ †	905	mocha brown
3799	m		/	236	grey
3823	V	N		386	lt yellow
3827	%	II		311	golden brown
518		•		1039	dk blue Fr. Knot

*Use **2** strands for Backstitch fish and **1** strand for all other.

† DMC 610 for spiral shell. DMC 612 for shell in border. DMC 3031 for base.

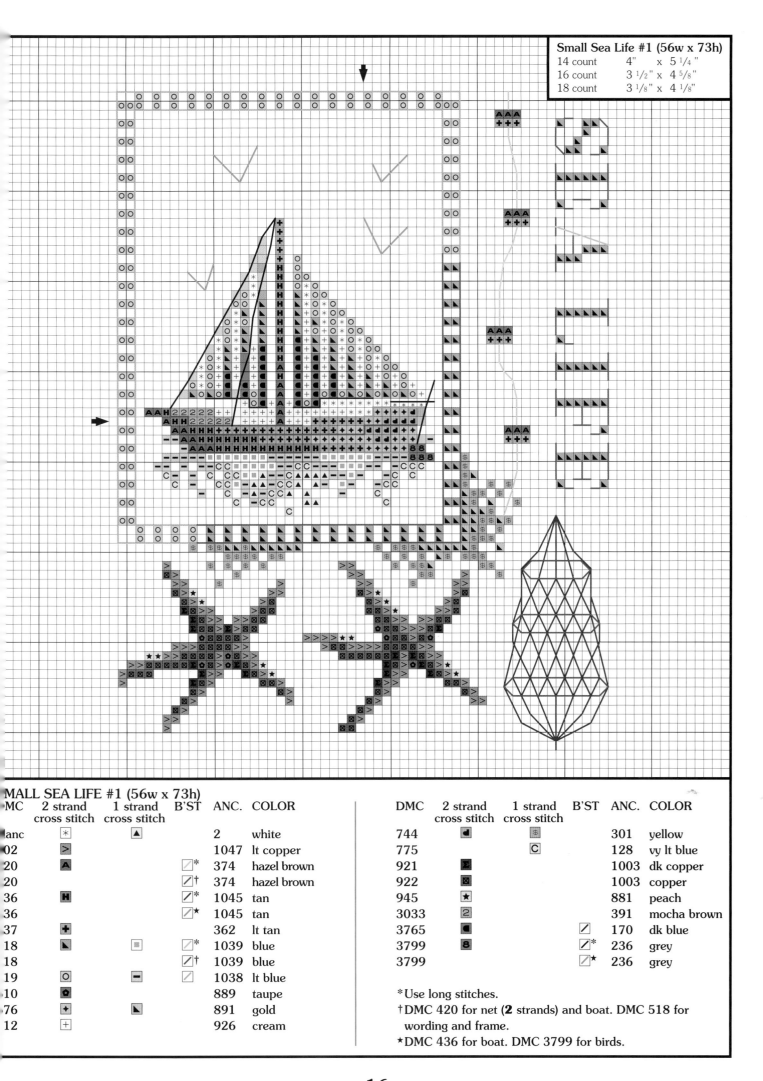

MALL SEA LIFE #1 (56w x 73h)

MC	2 strand cross stitch	1 strand cross stitch	B'ST	ANC.	COLOR	DMC	2 strand cross stitch	1 strand cross stitch	B'ST	ANC.	COLOR
anc	＊	▲		2	white	744	◤	⑤		301	yellow
02	＞			1047	lt copper	775		C		128	vy lt blue
20	A		◿＊	374	hazel brown	921	Σ			1003	dk copper
20			◿†	374	hazel brown	922	⊠			1003	copper
36	H		◿＊	1045	tan	945	★			881	peach
36			◿★	1045	tan	3033	②			391	mocha brown
37	＋			362	lt tan	3765	◖		◿	170	dk blue
18	◣	▣	◿＊	1039	blue	3799	⑧		◿＊	236	grey
18			◿†	1039	blue	3799			◿★	236	grey
19	○	—	◿	1038	lt blue						
10	⬢			889	taupe	*Use long stitches.						
76	✦	◥		891	gold	†DMC 420 for net (**2** strands) and boat. DMC 518 for						
12	＋			926	cream	wording and frame.						
						★DMC 436 for boat. DMC 3799 for birds.						

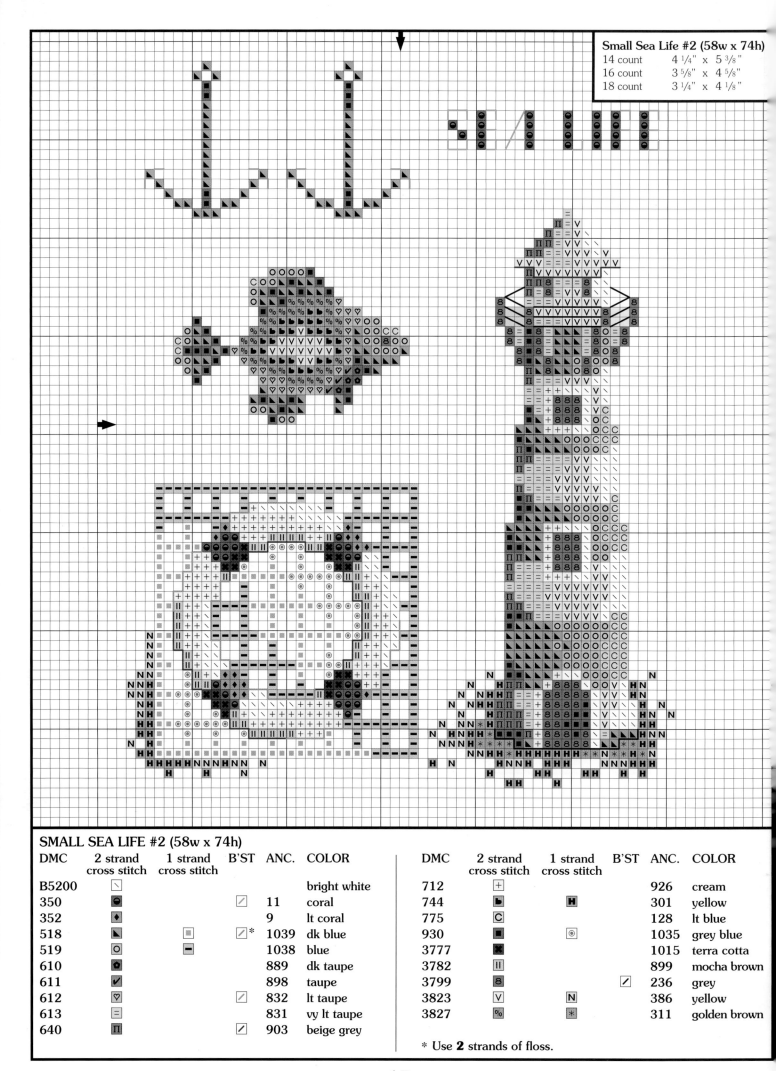

Small Sea Life #2 (58w x 74h)

14 count	4 ¼" x 5 ⅜"
16 count	3 ⅝" x 4 ⅝"
18 count	3 ¼" x 4 ⅛"

SMALL SEA LIFE #2 (58w x 74h)

DMC	2 strand cross stitch	1 strand cross stitch	B'ST	ANC.	COLOR	DMC	2 strand cross stitch	1 strand cross stitch	B'ST	ANC.	COLOR
B5200	◣				bright white	712	+			926	cream
350	◖		◢	11	coral	744	◖	H		301	yellow
352	◆			9	lt coral	775	C			128	lt blue
518	◣	◼	◢*	1039	dk blue	930	■	◉		1035	grey blue
519	O	−		1038	blue	3777	✖			1015	terra cotta
610	◉			889	dk taupe	3782	‖			899	mocha brown
611	✔			898	taupe	3799	8		◢	236	grey
612	♡		◢	832	lt taupe	3823	V	N		386	yellow
613	=			831	vy lt taupe	3827	%	*		311	golden brown
640	Π		◢	903	beige grey						

* Use **2** strands of floss.

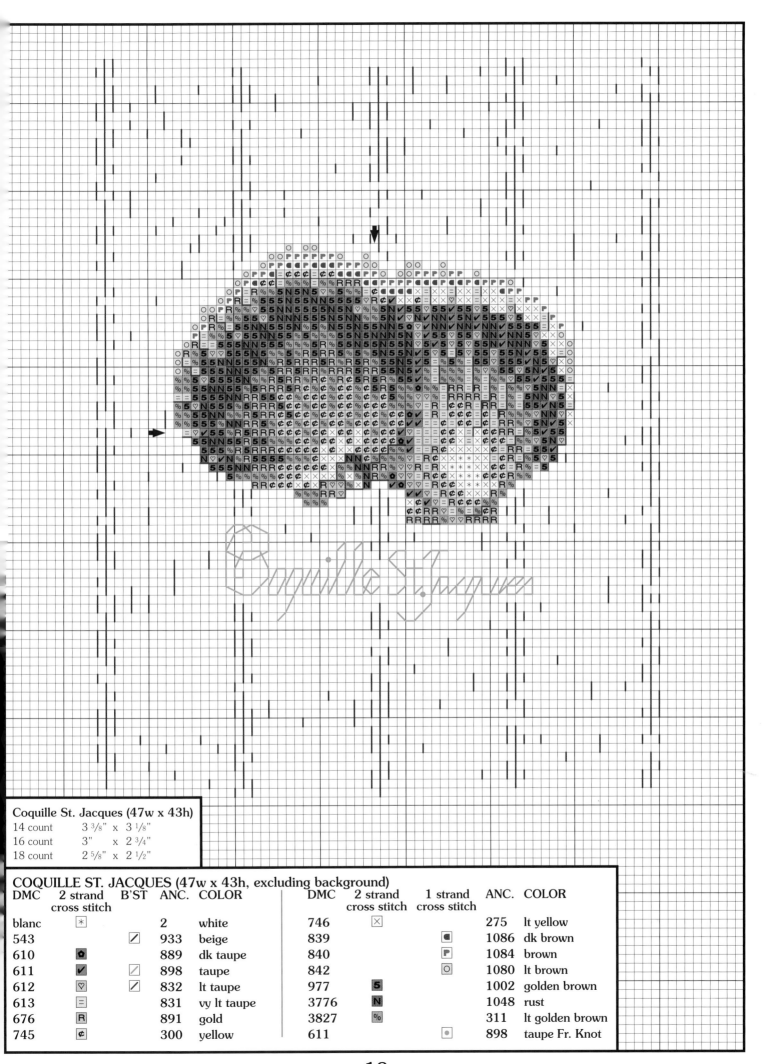

Coquille St. Jacques (47w x 43h)

14 count	3 ³/₈"	x	3 ¹/₈"
16 count	3"	x	2 ³/₄"
18 count	2 ⁵/₈"	x	2 ¹/₂"

COQUILLE ST. JACQUES (47w x 43h, excluding background)

DMC	2 strand cross stitch	B'ST	ANC.	COLOR	DMC	2 strand cross stitch	1 strand cross stitch	ANC.	COLOR
blanc	✳		2	white	746	⊠		275	lt yellow
543		⟋	933	beige	839		◨	1086	dk brown
610	⬠		889	dk taupe	840		ℙ	1084	brown
611	✔	⟋	898	taupe	842		⊙	1080	lt brown
612	♡	⟋	832	lt taupe	977	5		1002	golden brown
613	=		831	vy lt taupe	3776	N		1048	rust
676	R		891	gold	3827	%		311	lt golden brown
745	¢		300	yellow	611		•	898	taupe Fr. Knot

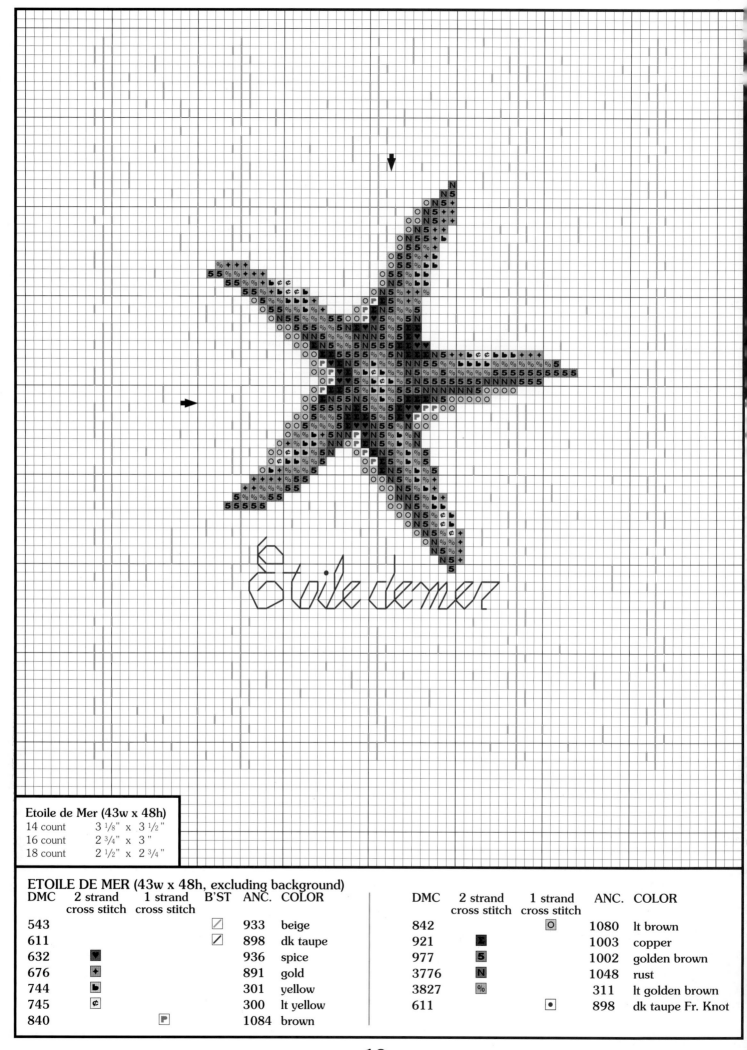

Etoile de Mer (43w x 48h)

14 count	3 1/8"	x	3 1/2"
16 count	2 3/4"	x	3"
18 count	2 1/2"	x	2 3/4"

ETOILE DE MER (43w x 48h, excluding background)

DMC	2 strand cross stitch	1 strand cross stitch	B'ST	ANC.	COLOR	DMC	2 strand cross stitch	1 strand cross stitch	ANC.	COLOR
543			⟋	933	beige	842		O	1080	lt brown
611			⟋	898	dk taupe	921	■		1003	copper
632	▼			936	spice	977	5		1002	golden brown
676	✦			891	gold	3776	N		1048	rust
744	►			301	yellow	3827	%		311	lt golden brown
745	¢			300	lt yellow	611		•	898	dk taupe Fr. Knot
840		P		1084	brown					

Working over Two Fabric Threads

When working over two fabric threads, the stitches should be placed so that vertical fabric threads support each stitch. Make sure that the first Cross Stitch is placed on the fabric with stitch 1-2 beginning and ending where a vertical fabric thread crosses over a horizontal fabric thread *(Fig. 7)*.

Fig. 7

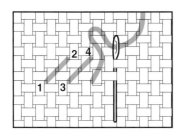

Project Information

Front Cover

All designs were stitched on 28 count Antique White Monaco over two fabric threads. One and two strands of floss were used for Cross Stitch. One strand was used for Backstitch and French Knots except where noted in key.

Large Sea Life — stitched on a 14" x 17" piece of Monaco (design size 8" x 10⁵/₈"; chart pgs. 7 & 8). It was custom framed using East Side Mouldings, Item #2200VB (opening size 9¹/₄" x 11¹/₂").

Fish Collage — stitched on a 10" x 11¹/₂" piece of Monaco (design size 3⁷/₈" x 5¹/₈"; chart pg. 15). It was custom framed using East Side Mouldings, Item #OCVB (opening size 5" x 6").

Fishing Boat #2 — stitched on a 12¹/₂" x 12¹/₂" piece of Monaco (design size 6¹/₈" x 6¹/₈"; chart pg. 10). It was custom framed using East Side Mouldings, Item #2200VB (opening size 7" x 7").

Back Cover

All designs were stitched on 28 count Antique White Monaco over two fabric threads. One and two strands of floss were used for Cross Stitch. One strand was used for Backstitch and French Knots except where noted in key.

Mouettes — stitched on a 12" x 11¹/₂" piece of Monaco (design size 5⁷/₈" x 5¹/₂", excluding background; chart pg. 11). We continued stitching the vertical background stitches to fill our frame. It was custom framed using East Side Mouldings, Item #TCW-1¹/₂" (opening size 6³/₄" x 7¹/₄").

Sterne — stitched on a 12¹/₂" x 11" piece of Monaco (design size 6³/₈" x 5", excluding background; chart pg. 12). We continued stitching the vertical background stitches to fill our frame. It was custom framed using East Side Mouldings, Item #TCW-1¹/₂" (opening size 7¹/₄" x 6¹/₄").

Etoile de Mer and **Coquille St. Jacques** — each stitched on a 9¹/₂" x 9¹/₂" piece of Monaco (approximate design size 3³/₈" x 3¹/₂" each, excluding background; charts pgs. 19 and 18). We continued stitching the vertical background stitches to fill our frames. They were custom framed using East Side Mouldings, Item #703SA (opening size 5¹/₂" x 5¹/₂").

Sea Horse and Shells — part of design from the Large Sea Life Collage (refer to photo) was stitched on a 10" x 10¹/₂" piece of Monaco (design size 4" x 4¹/₈"; chart pgs. 7 & 8). It was custom framed using East Side Mouldings, Item #2100WT (opening size 4³/₄" x 4¹/₂"). We glued small shells to jute cord and hung them from the right corner of the frame.

Page 2

Framed designs — each stitched on 28 count Antique White Monaco over two fabric threads. One and two strands of floss were used for Cross Stitch. One strand was used for Backstitch and French Knots except where noted in key.

Fishing Boats #1 and **#2** — each stitched on a 12¹/₂" x 12¹/₂" piece of Monaco (design size 6¹/₈" x 6¹/₈" each; charts pgs. 9 & 10). They were custom framed using East Side Mouldings, Item #2200VB (opening sizes 7" x 7").

Afghan — cut off selvages from an 18 count White Anne Cloth afghan. Fabric should measure 45"w x 58"l. Measure 5¹/₂" from raw edge of fabric and pull out one fabric thread. Fringe fabric up to missing thread. Repeat for each side. Tie an overhand knot at each corner with 4 horizontal and 4 vertical fabric threads. Working from corners, use 8 fabric threads for each knot until all threads are knotted.

Referring to diagram, stitch **Mouettes** (design size 9¹/₈" x 8¹/₂"; chart pg. 11) over two fabric threads, using three and six strands for Cross Stitch. Use two strands for Backstitch and four strands for French Knots. We did not stitch the word or any vertical background stitches on the afghan.

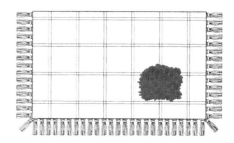

Page 3

All designs were stitched on 28 count Monaco over two fabric threads. One and two strands of floss were used for Cross Stitch. One strand was used for Backstitch and French Knots except where noted in key.

Three Shells — three shells only from Sea Horse Collage were stitched on a $14^1/2$" x 14" piece of Antique White Monaco (design size $2^1/4$" x $1^3/8$"; chart pg. 6). It was custom framed using East Side Mouldings, Item #2100WT (opening size $10^1/2$" x 10").

Pillow — lighthouse only from Large Sea Life stitched on an $8^1/2$" x 12" piece of Tea Dyed Monaco (design size $3^1/4$" x 6"; chart pgs. 7 & 8). Boat only from Fishing Boat #2 stitched on a 11" x 12" piece of Glass Blue Monaco (design size $5^5/8$" x $5^1/2$"; chart pg. 10).

When making pillow, always match right sides and raw edges and use a $1/2$" seam allowance.
1. Trim lighthouse stitched piece to 6"w x $9^1/2$"h. Trim boat stitched piece to $8^1/2$"w x $9^1/2$"h. For back, cut a piece of fabric $13^1/2$"w x $9^1/2$"h.
2. Referring to photo, sew stitched pieces together along side edges. Press seam allowances open. Sew front to back, leaving an opening for turning. Trim corners diagonally, turn right side out, and press.
3. Stuff pillow with polyester fiberfill; slipstitch opening closed.

Sea Horse Collage, Fish Collage, Small Sea Life #2, and **Small Sea Life #1** — each stitched on a 10" x 11" piece of Antique White Monaco (approximate design size 4" x 5"; charts pgs. 6, 15, 16, & 17). They were custom framed using East Side Mouldings, Item #OCVB (opening sizes 5" x 6").

Page 4

All designs were stitched on a 28 count Monaco over two fabric threads. One and two strands of floss were used for Cross Stitch. One strand was **used** for Backstitch except where noted in key.

Red Lighthouse, Blue Lighthouse, Trumpet Shell, Chambered Nautilus, Blue Sailboat, and **Brown Sailboat** — each stitched on an 6" x 6" piece of Antique White Monaco (approximate design size 2" x 2"; charts pgs. 13 & 14). They were custom framed using East Side Mouldings, Item #2100WT (opening sizes 4" x 4").

Pillow — Fishing Boat #1 stitched on a $12^1/2$" x $12^1/2$" piece of Tea Dyed Monaco (design size $6^1/8$" x $6^1/8$"; chart pg. 9).

When making pillow decoration, always match right sides and raw edges and use a $1/2$" seam allowance.
1. Trim stitched piece to $9^1/4$"w x $9^1/4$"h. For back, cut a piece of fabric same size as front. Sew front to back, leaving an opening for turning. Trim corners diagonally, turn right side out, and press. Slipstitch opening closed.
2. Tack corners of stitched piece to the front of a purchased pillow. Glue a shell in each corner of stitched piece.

Shadow Box — fish on stand only from Fish Collage was stitched on a $6^1/8$" x $8^1/8$" piece of Antique White Monaco (design size $3^3/8$" x $3^3/4$"; chart pg. 15). Place top of design $1^3/4$" from one short edge of fabric. It was placed in an 8" x 10" purchased shadow box.

1. Fringe $3/8$" on all sides. Trim edges evenly.
2. Cut a piece of mat board 8" x 10" to fit shadow box. Center and attach stitched piece to mat board using double-sided tape.
3. Glue an assortment of shells in shadow box. Insert mat board into shadow box.

Page 5

Framed designs and **Scrapbook** were stitched on 28 count Antique White Monaco over two fabric threads. One and two strands of floss were used for Cross Stitch. One strand was used for Backstitch except where noted in key.

Quad Frame — **Small Sea Life #1, Small Sea Life #2, Fish Collage,** and **Sea Horse Collage** were each stitched on a 10" x 11" piece of Monaco (approximate design size 4" x 5" each; charts pgs. 16, 17, 15, & 6). Each design was custom framed using East Side Mouldings, Item #3100VB (opening sizes $4^1/2$" x $5^3/4$"). Frames were joined on back using 2" mending plates.

Scrapbook — Small Sea Life #2 was stitched on a $10^1/2$" x $11^1/2$" piece of Monaco (design size $4^1/4$" x $5^3/8$"; chart pg. 17), made into a padded shape and glued to a purchased scrapbook.

1. To make a padded shape, trim stitched piece to desired finished size plus 1" on all sides. Cut one piece each of batting and lightweight cardboard the desired finished size. Glue batting to cardboard. Center cardboard (batting side down) on wrong side of stitched piece. Fold fabric over edges of cardboard; glue.
2. Center and glue padded shape to front of purchased scrapbook.
3. Cut a length of jute cord the same measurement as outer edge of padded shape plus 6". Beginning and ending 3" from ends, glue trim to padded shape along outer edge; tie ends in a square knot. Glue shells to scrapbook.

Address Book — part of Small Sea Life #1 (refer to photo) was stitched on the 5" x 7" insert of 14 count White Vinyl-Weave™ (design size $3^3/8$" x $5^1/8$"; chart pg. 16) from a Crafter's Pride® Address Book. One and two strands of floss were used for Cross Stitch. One strand was used for Backstitch except where noted in key. To stitch on Vinyl-Weave, hold it flat; do not use a hoop. Stitch with a #7 sharp needle.

We have made every effort to ensure that these instructions are accurate and complete. We cannot, however, be responsible for human error, typographical mistakes, or variations in individual work.

Production Team: Writer – Karen Jackson; Artist – Karen F. Allbright; and Photo Stylists – Sondra Daniel and Karen Hall.

Instructions tested and some cover items made by Muriel Hicks, Arthur Jungnickel, Phyllis Lundy, Karen Matthew, Angie Perryman, Cynthia Sanders, Gail Sharp, Anne Simpson, Lavonne Sims, and Helen Stanton.